QUINTON DE KOCK

SOUTH AFRICAN CRICKETER

MR VIVEK KUMAR PANDEY SHAMBHUNATH

ISBN 979-888546361-4

Short biography of Quinton de Kock and about life.During writing this book no character & no religious are harmed written by Mr Vivek Kumar Pandey. winner youngest writer award 1st rank in india 2020.He is only one writer can publish 700+ own book that was greatest successfull in his life .

Contents

Foreword

Author biography in English :MY NAME IS VIVEK KUMAR PANDEY . I WAS BORN IN 30 SEP 2002,I AM FROM SURAT GUJARAT INDIA.MY DREAM WAS TO BE GOOD WRITERS ,MY FAMILY SUPPORTED ME TO SUCCESSFUL AND I CAN DO IT MY SELF.How do I write? That is a question, I believe, that cannot be honestly answered by me."CELEBRATING YOUNGEST WRITER AWARD WINNER IN GUJARAT 1ST RANK" MR PANDEY JI . I may think I did a good job writing something when in reality it could be horrible. The reader is the one who decides the quality of my writing. I do not find writing to be natural to me and therefore find it to be a real challenge. My trick as a challenged writer is to do the best I can and know that I am happy with the final outcome. It may take a while to do my best and there may be quite a few problems I run into along the way.

I am not a greedy person those who are thinking about me and my self I never tried it anyone people suffering from sadness ,I trying to get promoted people suffering from happiness and joy in your Life Time. Now in current situation in India and also world people are unemployed and have no many but our indian governor help to people to get free food from ration card , i also take part in leadership team ,i am Motivational speaker , Film script writer. There was my two dream firstly writer and secondly actor & also my own film is upcoming soon i done almost completely completed script for my film .I AM GOING TO SAY WORD OF HEART TOUCH OUT PLEASE READ IT" , firstly i thanks my father he supports me in this field they always getting inspired me by own his words and behavior ,they always said that he was a biggest person in the world in future and also they purchase fruit and chocolate for me in anytime & anyway , firstly my father buy him then call me Vivek you want a chocolate i will say yes papa but how many tell me ,papa: you tell me how much i buy him i told 1 or 2 chocolate but my father purchase whole the boxes of chocolate and they get suprised me. MY FATHER WAS BORN IN " 20 SEPTEMBER" 1971 IN INDIA.

1) MY FATHER FAVORITE CLOTHES IS KURTA PAIJMA AND ALSO STYLES SHOE

2) FAVORITE SINGER IS KISHORE DA

3) FAVORITE STATE GUJARAT AND KOLKATA , HIS VILLAGE IN BIHAR

4) FAVORITE COLOR BLACK AND WHITE

THEY ALSO LOVE cricket like IPL and one day t-20 .they also like watching a News daily and heard the song daily ,they also interested in tik tok video but in current time tik tok is banned in india but also few videos are in you tube. In lockdown time my family and me very enjoy day daily. my father play daily ludo with his sister and son, daughter.they always loved tea and coffee anytime call me "। वविके थोडा़ चाय बनाओना वविके तमु्हारे हाथ का चाय अच्छा लगता है". I make it tea for my father but some reason after the April to june they are suffering from fever and cough , weakness on 6 June 2020 my father death. they not told me say bye bye his life. After death of 6 June on 10 june my mom and dad anniversary.but my father is Best in the world they can do anything for me please take care of father and respect it of your parents.

CHAPTER ONE

Quinton de Kock

- Quinton de Kock

1. During writing this book no character & no religious are harmed written by Mr Vivek Kumar Pandey.

Quinton de Kock (born 17 December 1992) is a South African cricketer and former captain of the Proteas in all three formats. He currently plays for the Titans at the domestic level, Mumbai Indians in the Indian Premier League, and South Africa at international level. He was named the Cricketer of the Year at Cricket South Africa's 2017 Annual Awards.

An opening batsman and wicket-keeper, de Kock made his domestic debut for the Highveld Lions during the 2012/2013 season. He quickly caught the national selectors' eye when he starred in a match-winning partnership with Neil McKenzie in the Champions League T20 against the Mumbai Indians in the Indian Premier League (IPL). He also finished fourth on the first-class rankings, despite playing only six of the 10 matches that summer.

He made his international debut in the first match of South Africa's home Twenty20 International series against the touring New Zealanders during the 2012/13 season. He was asked to keep wickets in place of AB de Villiers, who asked to be rested. He has since played regularly for the team at both One Day International (ODI) and Twenty20 International (T20I) level. In February 2014, he also made his Test debut for South Africa, playing solely as a batsman.

By his 20th ODI match, he had already scored five centuries. He became the fourth player to score three successive one-day centuries and the second player to score four ODI centuries before his 21st birthday. In his 74th ODI, against Sri Lanka on 10 February 2017, he became the fastest player to complete 12 ODI hundreds, bettering Hashim Amla, who had achieved the landmark in 81 innings.

Before joining the Titans in 2015, de Kock played domestic cricket for Gauteng and the Highveld Lions. He has also played in the Indian Premier League (IPL) for Sunrisers Hyderabad, Delhi Daredevils, Royal Challengers Bangalore, and Mumbai Indians. Although he opens the batting in One Day International and T20 cricket, he primarily bats in the middle order in Test cricket. In July 2020, he was named South Africa's Men's Cricketer of the Year at Cricket South Africa's annual awards ceremony.In December 2020, in the series against Sri Lanka, de Kock captained South Africa for the first time in Test cricket.

- *Early career*

De Kock attended King Edward VII School in Johannesburg. He was spotted as a schoolboy talent and used to play for the affiliate club Old Eds. In the 2012 ICC Under-19 Cricket World Cup, he scored 95 off 131 balls in South Africa's first match against Bangladesh, which the team won by 133 runs. In the second match against Namibia, he scored 126 off 106 balls, with South Africa winning again, by 209 runs. In the quarter-final match against England, de Kock scored only 7 runs, but performed well as wicket-keeper, recording five dismissals (two stumpings and three catches). Overall, de Kock scored 284 runs throughout the tournament, ranking fourth for the tournament.

"*Domestic career*"

From Johannesburg, he debuted for Gauteng's senior team during the 2009–10 season, aged 16, and subsequently represented the national under-19 team at the 2012 Under-19 World Cup. In April 2021, he was named in Northerns' squad, ahead of the 2021–22 cricket season in South Africa.

- *Ram Slam Twenty20*

In the 2013 domestic twenty20 tournament in South Africa, De Kock played several good knocks to take his team Highveld Lions to the final where they won, eventually becoming the season dalla champions. On 18 February 2013, in the same tournament against Cape Cobras he hit the second highest T20 score of 126 in South Africa. His knock of 126 is also the highest T20 score ever made by a wicketkeeper batsman in an innings (126).

- Indian Premier League

De Kock was bought for $20,000 by IPL franchise Sunrisers Hyderabad in the IPL players' auction on 3 February 2013 to play for the 2013 IPL Season. But he failed to impress in IPL-6 when he got chances in the Sunrisers Hyderabad squad. In the Indian Premier League (IPL), de Kock spent the 2013 tournament with Sunrisers Hyderabad, and signed to the Delhi Daredevils for the 2014 tournament. On 12 February 2014, De Koçk was sold to Delhi Daredevils for Rs 3.5 Crore (approximately $560,000 according to the then exchange rate) in the IPL players' auction. He eventually became the highest bid foreign wicket-keeper in the auction. He was a part of the Delhi Daredevils team till 2017. He was bought by Royal Challengers Bangalore in 2018 auction for Rs 2.8 Crore. He played for Mumbai Indians in the 2019 Season after MI purchased him from Royal Challengers Bangalore where he played some crucial knocks throughout the tournament which saw Mumbai win the 2019 Final against Chennai Super Kings. He was the highest run scorer for the Mumbai Indians in the 2019 IPL season.

- *Other T20 franchise cricket*

De Kock came to the spotlight after scoring 51 not out off 33 balls in their first match for South African Highveld Lions against Mumbai Indians in Champions League Twenty20, 2012 in Johannesburg. While chasing 158, after an early breakdown, he along with the experienced Neil McKenzie took the team home.Although he failed to keep this consistency in the remaining matches, he came to the spotlight after this tournament. In the 2013 CLT20 which was hosted in India, de Kock scored 109 not out off 63 balls against Otago Volts in Jaipur, Rajasthan.

In October 2018, he was named in Cape Town Blitz's squad for the first edition of the Mzansi Super League T20 tournament.In September 2019, he was named in the squad for the Cape Town Blitz team for the 2019 Mzansi Super League tournament.

- *International career*

- ODI cricket

De Kock represented South Africa for the first time, at T20 level, on 21 December 2012 against New Zealand. While South Africa crushed New Zealand and got them all out for only 86, the hosts chased it down easily with 8 wickets still remaining. De Kock made an impression on his first appearance by scoring an unbeaten 28 off 23 while chasing. He also kept wicket and gloved two catches. De Kock made his debut for the South African ODI side on 19 January 2013, against New Zealand at Boland Park Stadium, Paarl, South Africa.It was reported that he was training and grooming under veteran retired South African wicket-keeper batsman Mark Boucher ahead of the ODI series against New Zealand. He was promoted to the opening batting spot from his second match onwards with Graeme Smith in his debut series.

In November 2013, he was selected in the first XI of South Africa against Pakistan in the United Arab Emirates, in place of

Colin Ingram. De Kock scored a match winning 112 off 135 balls on a tough batting track in Abu Dhabi in the fourth ODI to reach his maiden ODI century. South Africa won the ODI series 4–1. They also played two T20 games against Pakistan. De Kock scored 48 not out in the first match while chasing and took them home. They won that T20 series too by 2–0.

- On 5 December 2013, De Kock scored 135 against India at his home ground in Johannesburg. His innings guided the team to a 141-run victory over India and he was awarded his first-ever 'Man of the Match' award in One Day International cricket.He followed his performance with another successive ODI ton in the next match against the same team in Durban. He scored 106 runs making a record-breaking opening stand of 194 in Durban with teammate Hashim Amla who also scored a century in the same match. This performance awarded him another 'Man of the Match' award while they already won the series beating India by 134 runs. He again broke a century knock of 101 in the 3rd ODI which was later abandoned due to rain, but he became only the fifth person to achieve this feat of three consecutive centuries in One Day Internationals, after Zaheer Abbas, Saeed Anwar, Herschelle Gibbs and AB de Villiers. He also became the highest run-getter ever in a three-match bilateral ODI series, breaking the previous record of Martin Guptill. Meanwhile, he was awarded the 'Man of the Series'.

De Kock scored his 5th ODI century knock of 128 against Sri Lanka to record their first-ever ODI series win in Sri Lanka. He also scored his maiden test fifty in the series.

In the 3-match tour to Zimbabwe in August, 2014, De Kock eventually became the joint quickest batsman to reach 1000 runs in ODI cricket sharing the record with Viv Richards, Jonathan Trott and Kevin Pietersen. He reached the milestone in 21 innings. He was also awarded the 'Player of the Series' in that tournament where South Africa beat Zimbabwe 3–0.

- For his performances in 2014, he was named in the World ODI XI by ICC. He was also named as wicket keeper of the ODI XI in 2016 by ICC and Cricinfo.

In the ODI series against Bangladesh in 2017, he along with Hashim Amla set the highest record ODI runstand for South Africa with an unbeaten partnership of 282 runs. This is also the highest-ever partnership in One-Day Internationals without losing any wickets.For his performances in 2017, he was named as wicket keeper of the World ODI XI by ICC.

In April 2019, he was named in South Africa's squad for the 2019 Cricket World Cup.The International Cricket Council (ICC) named de Kock as the key player of South Africa's squad for the tournament. In the opening match of the World Cup against England, he scored 68. He ultimately finished with 305 runs from 8 matches, including three half centuries.

On 4 February 2020, during the home ODI series against England he scored his 15th ODI century and became joint second fastest South African to reach 5,000 ODI runs.In the same match he also became only the second wicket keeper opening batsman after Adam Gilchrist while captaining the side to score a century in ODIs.

- *Test cricket*

In February 2014, de Kock made his Test debut for South Africa, scoring seven runs in the first innings and 34 runs in the second innings against Australia at St George's Oval in Port Elizabeth.

In January 2016, when South Africa was losing the home Test series against England, De Kock was recalled to the Test side for the second Test, taking the keeper's gloves from AB de Villiers, but failed to deliver. He was replaced by Dane Vilas at the 11th hour before the third Test, after a freak injury he picked up at home the afternoon before. He was again selected for the fourth and the final Test and scored his debut Test century with a score of 129 not out in the first innings coming to bat at number seven. In the tour, De

Kock reached a milestone as the fastest to reach 10 ODI centuries. He completed his 10th century in his 55th match. In their 3rd test against Pakistan he made his same score of 129 in their 2nd innings in 2019.

On 22 July 2018 during the second test match against Sri Lanka, he went on to become the fastest wicketkeeper in terms of matches (35) to take 150 test dismissals. On 27 January 2019 during the fourth test match against England, he broke the record for the fastest wicketkeeper to effect 200 dismissals (47).

On 12 June 2021, Quinton de Kock joined Mark Boucher in 3,000 runs in Test cricket as a wicketkeeper for South Africa club during his career-best 141 not-out against West Indies.

- *T20I cricket*

In March 2014, South Africa played a 3-match Twenty20 series against Australia. De Kock was named the 'Player of the Series' in the tournament although South Africa lost the series by 0–2.In 2019–2020 season de Kock was brilliant in this format scoring 4 half centuries. In September 2021, De Kock was named in South Africa's squad for the 2021 ICC Men's T20 World Cup.

In October 2021, during the Men's T20 World Cup, de Kock made himself unavailable for South Africa's match against West Indies after refusing to take the knee. Following the match, he apologised saying he would take the knee and wanted to play for his country again. De Kock explained that he had originally decided not to take the knee because of the way in which Cricket South Africa had handled the issue by mandating that all players take the knee shortly before the match against the West Indies. However, he returned to the side for South Africa's next match, against Sri Lanka, and took the knee before the start of play.

- Records and achievements

1. Fastest South African to reach 1,000 ODI runs.

2. Fastest wicketkeeper in terms of matches (35) to take 150 test dismissals.
3. Fastest wicket-keeper, in terms of matches, to complete 200 dismissals in Tests (47) beating the previous record held by Adam Gilchrist.
4. Only the second wicket keeper opener while captaining the side to score a century in ODIs.
5. Fastest South African to score a T20I half century (17 balls).

CHAPTER TWO

Currently Quinton de Kock Play With Csk

- Royal Challengers Bangalore

The Royal Challengers Bangalore (often abbreviated as RCB) are a franchise cricket team based in Bangalore, Karnataka, that plays in the Indian Premier League (IPL). It was founded in 2008 by United Spirits and named after the company's liquor brand Royal Challenge. Since its inception, the team has played its home matches at the M. Chinnaswamy Stadium.

The Royal Challengers have never won the IPL but finished runners-up on three occasions between 2009 and 2016. Their lack of success over the years despite the presence of various notable players has earned them the tag of "underachievers".The team holds the records of both the highest and the lowest totals in the IPL – 263/5 and 49 respectively.

- *Franchise history*

In September 2007, the Board of Control for Cricket in India (BCCI) announced the establishment of the Indian Premier League, a Twenty20 competition to be started in 2008. The teams for the competition, representing 8 different cities of India, including Bangalore, were put up on auction in Mumbai on 20 February 2008.

The Bangalore franchise was purchased by Vijay Mallya, who paid US$111.6 million for it. This was the second highest bid for a team, next only to Reliance Industries' bid of US$111.9 million for the Mumbai Indians.

The brand value of Royal Challengers Bangalore was estimated to be 595 crore (US$79 million) in 2019, according to a survey conducted by Duff & Phelps.

- *Team history*

Rahul Dravid was the team's icon player in 2008.

Ahead of the 2008 player auction, the IPL named Rahul Dravid as the icon player for the Bangalore franchise, which meant that Dravid would be paid 15% more than the highest bid player at the auction. The franchise acquired a number of Indian and international players at the auction such as Jacques Kallis, Anil Kumble, Zaheer Khan, Mark Boucher, Dale Steyn and Cameron White.

They also signed up Ross Taylor, Misbah-ul-Haq and India under-19 World Cup winning captain Virat Kohli in the second round of auction. The team won only 4 of the 14 matches in the inaugural season, finishing seventh in the eight-team table. Only Dravid managed to score more than 300 runs in the tournament and they had to even bench their costliest foreign player Kallis for a few of the matches due to his poor form. The string of failures midway through the season led to the sacking of the CEO Charu Sharma, who was replaced with Brijesh Patel.Team owner Vijay Mallya went on to publicly criticize Dravid and Sharma for the players selected by them at the auction and stated that his "biggest mistake was to abstain from the selection of the team."Eventually the chief cricketing officer Martin Crowe resigned.

At the 2009 player auction, the franchise signed up Kevin Pietersen for a record sum of US$1.55 million, making him the joint costliest player, along with fellow Englishman Andrew Flintoff who was signed up by the Chennai Super Kings for the same amount.

They also traded Zaheer Khan for Robin Uthappa with the Mumbai Indians and also roped in local batsman Manish Pandey from them. Ahead of the tournament, which was shifted to South Africa due to the general elections, the Royal Challengers named Pietersen as the team captain for the season. Bangalore continued to struggle during the initial games of the 2009 season, winning only two of their first six games under the new captain. However, the team's fortunes improved after Pietersen left for national duty and Kumble took over the captaincy, as the team went on to win six of their remaining eight league games to finish third on the points table. The team qualified for the semifinal where they faced the Super Kings. Electing to field first, Bangalore restricted their opponents to 146 and chased down the total with 5 wickets in hand, thanks to 48 and 44 by Pandey and Dravid respectively. In the final against Deccan Chargers, the Royal Challengers bowlers, led by Kumble's 4 for 16, kept the Chargers down to 143/6. However, they struggled in the runchase, with only four batsmen reaching double figures, and lost the match by six runs in a tense finish.Ross Taylor was one of the top performers for RCB in 2009 and 2010.

In 2010, the Royal Challengers continued under Kumble's captaincy and finished the regular season with seven wins from 14 matches and 14 points. They were one of the four teams tied on 14 points with two semifinal spots at stake; they qualified for the semifinal as their net run rate was superior to those of the Delhi Daredevils and the Kolkata Knight Riders. In the semifinal, the Royal Challengers were defeated by the table-toppers Mumbai Indians by 35 runs. With a convincing nine-wicket win over defending champions Deccan Chargers in the third-place playoff, the Royal Challengers qualified for the 2010 Champions League Twenty20. Kumble retired at the conclusion of the Champions League, having led the team to the semifinals of both the IPL and the CLT20 that year.

- *2011–2017 Gayle-Kohli-de Villiers era*

On 8 January 2011, the IPL Governing Council held the auction for the fourth season of the league. The franchises had the option of retaining a maximum of four players for a sum of US$4.5 million. However, Royal Challengers retained only one of their players, Virat Kohli, leaving the rest of the players back in the auction pool. When other IPL franchises let go the non-performers from each of their teams, RCB lost the top performers from the previous season by releasing them back to the auction pool. On Day-One of the auction, Bangalore bought Sri Lankan Tillakaratne Dilshan for $650,000, their former player and Mumbai Indians spearhead Zaheer Khan for $900,000, ace middle order batsman AB de Villiers for $1.1 million, former New Zealand skipper Daniel Vettori for $550,000, India's new sensation, who played with Mumbai Indians until last season, Saurabh Tiwary for a whopping $1.6 million, Australia's Dirk Nannes for $650,000 and India's young talent Cheteshwar Pujara for $700,000. West Indian batsman Chris Gayle was brought in as a replacement for the injured Dirk Nannes in the middle of the tournament. Vettori led the side for the fourth season of the IPL.

RCB kicked off their campaign with a comfortable six-wicket win over the newly formed team, Kochi Tuskers Kerala. But then, they suffered three big defeats at the hands of Mumbai Indians, Deccan Chargers and Chennai Super Kings. At this stage, speedster Dirk Nannes was ruled out of the tournament and the RCB team management named West Indian opener Chris Gayle as his replacement. Gayle started off the tournament with a century (102* off 55 balls) against Kolkata Knight Riders, giving the Challengers an emphatic 9-wicket win. RCB also managed to beat Delhi Daredevils and Pune Warriors in their next two matches. They went on to beat Kings XI Punjab by a big margin of 85 runs, after Gayle smashed his second century of the tournament (107 off 49 balls).

- They won their next two matches against Kochi and Rajasthan Royals, both comprehensively by 9 wickets. They also defeated

Kolkata in a rain-affected match at Bangalore. But then, Kings XI Punjab, riding on a blistering hundred by their skipper Adam Gilchrist, ended RCB's 7-match winning streak, with a huge 111-run margin win. In their last league match, the Challengers beat the defending champions Chennai Super Kings by 8 wickets to end at the top of the points table. Chris Gayle, shining once again with the bat, scored an unbeaten 75 off 50 balls.

Royal Challengers faced Chennai Super Kings in the 1st qualifier at Mumbai. Virat Kohli scored an unbeaten 70 off just 44 balls to help RCB put up 175/4 in their 20 overs. Despite losing early wickets, Chennai went on to win the match by 6 wickets. The win took Chennai to the final and RCB faced Mumbai Indians in the 2nd qualifier in Chennai. Batting first, Royal Challengers made a massive 185/4 in 20 overs on a slow Chepauk track. Chris Gayle was the star once again for them as he scored a blistering 89 runs off 47 balls. Mumbai never looked in the hunt for a win as they collapsed to a 43-run defeat. The Royal Challengers qualified for the final with this win and went on to face Chennai at their home ground in the final. Winning the toss, Chennai elected to bat first in the final. The Super Kings posted a huge total of 205/5. The Challengers did not bat well and lost the match by 58 runs. Chris Gayle was named Man of the Tournament and Bangalore set a new IPL record for the most successive wins by winning 7 matches on the trot.

- Royal Challengers Bangalore qualified for the main event of the 2011 Champions League Twenty20 as they finished runners-up in the 2011 Indian Premier League, this made the Challengers the first and only team ever to play in all the three seasons of the tournament. The Challengers, placed in Group B in the first round of the tournament, kicked off their quest for glory with a last-ball defeat to the Warriors. They suffered a big 9-wicket defeat at the hands of the IPL counterparts Kolkata Knight Riders in their second group match, leaving them with two must-win matches in order to qualify for the semi-finals. They registered their first win in the competition, in an emphatic manner, by beating Somerset by 51 runs, thanks to Chris Gayle's 46-ball 86.

The win also consolidated their poor net run-rate. In their last group match, they faced the champions from Australia, the Southern Redbacks. Batting first, the Redbacks rode on a century by Daniel Harris (108* from 61 balls) to set RCB a target of 215. The Royal Challengers came out with a spirited batting performance with Tillakaratne Dilshan and Virat Kohli scoring half-centuries. However, the Redbacks hampered the run-chase by picking up wickets at regular stages towards the end of the innings. With six runs required off the last ball to win the match, RCB found an unlikely-hero in Arun Karthik, who struck Daniel Christian for a six over deep mid-wicket, to take RCB through to the semi-finals. The Challengers, despite being level on points with Kolkata Knight Riders and Warriors, qualified for the semi-finals on basis of having a better net run-rate than the two teams.

- The Royal Challengers played the New South Wales Blues in the semi-finals of the tournament. Winning the toss, Daniel Vettori put the Blues in to bat and the decision seemed to backfire as the Blues amassed 203/2 in 20 overs, mainly due to the efforts of David Warner who struck an unbeaten 123 off just 68 balls. Despite losing Dilshan early in the chase, RCB got off to a rollicking start with Chris Gayle smashing 92 runs from only 41 deliveries. He was ably supported by Kohli, who struck an unbeaten 84 from 49 balls to give RCB a comfortable 6-wicket victory with 9 balls to spare. They took on an injury-hit Mumbai Indians in the final at Chennai. Mumbai winning the toss, chose to bat and put up a modest total of 139 in 20 overs. After getting off to a blistering start with the bat, the Challengers lost wickets at regular intervals before getting bundled out for 108 in 19.2 overs, falling short of the target by 31 runs. Mumbai skipper

Harbhajan Singh was awarded the Man of the Match for picking 3/20 in his four overs.

In the pre-season transfer window, Royal Challengers Bangalore transferred Australian all-rounder Andrew McDonald from Delhi Daredevils. RCB paid US$100,000 as transferred fees. Royal Challengers Bangalore also retained Chris Gayle for the next two IPL seasons.

Before the 2012 auction, RCB had got Andrew McDonald transferred from Delhi Daredevils. They had also bought out the contracts of Johan Van der Wath, Jonathan Vandiar and Nuwan Pradeep. In the auction, RCB bought only Vinay Kumar for $1 million and Muttiah Muralitharan for $220,200.

Royal Challengers Bangalore began the 2012 IPL without the services of talisman Chris Gayle who had arrived in India, carrying a groin injury he had sustained in the preceding Bangladesh Premier League. Sreenath Aravind, RCB's most successful bowler in 2011 too was laid low by injury and Harshal Patel emerged as the preferred third seamer in the side ahead of Abhimanyu Mithun. AB de Villiers and Muttiah Muralitharan gave the team a winning start against Delhi but 3 consecutive losses followed. The team rallied back, Chris Gayle finding his touch to hit 5 consecutive sixes off Rahul Sharma and Saurabh Tiwary hitting a six off the last ball to win the team a tight chase against Pune. Gayle shone again at Mohali in a comprehensive win while de Villiers, Tillakaratne Dilshan and KP Appanna engineered another win in Jaipur. A washed out match at Bangalore against Chennai denied the team a chance at gaining 2 points outright, the teams sharing points 1-1 each.

- Two subsequent losses put RCB in competition with Rajasthan Royals, Chennai Super Kings and Kings XI Punjab for the last play-offs slot. Daniel Vettori benched himself so the team could play Muttiah Muralitharan as one of the four foreigners allowed in the playing XI, Virat Kohli taking up the captaincy duties. The team signed Prasanth Parameswaran, who played for Kochi

Tuskers Kerala in the 2011 IPL, as a replacement for the injured Sreenath Aravind. A spectacular chase against Deccan Chargers at Bangalore and two routs in Mumbai and Pune put the team back on track for a place in the play-offs. RCB went down to Mumbai in a hard-fought match at Bangalore but bounced back in Delhi as Chris Gayle became the first man to hit 3 centuries in the IPL, hitting 128* at Delhi.

Other results in the tournament now placed RCB in direct competition with Chennai for the final play-offs slot. The teams were tied on points with Chennai ahead on net run-rate but RCB had a game in hand while Chennai had played out their games. A batting failure at Hyderabad in RCB's final game of the season led to the end of the team's 2012 campaign, making it the first time since 2009 that they failed to qualify for both the play-offs and the Champions League Twenty20. Chris Gayle was the highest run scorer of the tournament for the second year in a row, scoring 733 runs at 61.08 with 7 fifties, 1 hundred and a strike rate of 160.74. Vinay Kumar finished as the 5th highest wicket taker of the tournament with his 19 wickets from 17 matches.

Before the 2013 auction, RCB released Mohammad Kaif, Charl Langeveldt, Dirk Nannes, Luke Pomersbach and Rilee Rossouw. At the auction, RCB bought Christopher Barnwell, Daniel Christian, Moisés Henriques, Ravi Rampaul, Pankaj Singh, R. P. Singh and Jaydev Unadkat. RCB kicked off their 2013 campaign by winning their first 6 home games, starting with a 2-run win over Mumbai Indians where Chris Gayle scored 92* off 58 balls and Vinay Kumar picking up 3 wickets. But they suffered a super-over defeat to the newly formed Sunrisers Hyderabad but then they beat the same opponents convincingly by 6 wickets where Virat Kohli smashed a brilliant 93*. They also beat Kolkata Knight Riders by 8 wickets. Gayle and Kohli were in a tremendous form with the bat while Vinay Kumar was the hero with the ball. RCB suffered a shock in the next match against Chennai Super Kings where R. P. Singh conceded a no-ball on the last ball of the match which was a catch.

- However, the team rallied back to win their next 3 games. One of the matches against Pune Warriors India saw Chris Gayle smash 175 off just 66 balls which was the highest individual score in T20 cricket and RCB put up 263-5 which was the highest total in T20 cricket. Pune never fought back in the chase and eventually lost the match by 130 runs. People often nicknamed Bangalore as "Ban-gayle-ore". However, the team began to lose matches away from home. One of the matches against Punjab saw David Miller score 101 off just 38 balls to guide Punjab to an unlikely victory. RCB only managed to beat Pune Warriors India and Delhi Daredevils away from home. They were now in direct competition with Sunrisers Hyderabad with 16 points from 13 matches who were also with 16 points from 13 matches. A batting failure against Kolkata and a poor fielding and bowling performance against Punjab at Bangalore left RCB in a do or die situation in their last league match against Chennai Super Kings at Bangalore. Fortunately, RCB registered a stunning win in their last match which was affected by rain. Now, RCB could only qualify for the playoffs if Kolkata would beat Hyderabad. Unfortunately, Sunrisers Hyderabad won the match convincingly by 5 wickets which ended RCB's 2013 campaign. Chris Gayle was the leading run scorer for the team, scoring 708 runs and Vinay Kumar was the leading wicket taker by taking 22 wickets.

Virat Kohli was named the captain of RCB team. Before the 2014 auction, AB de Villiers, Chris Gayle and Virat Kohli were retained from the previous seasons. The players bought in the 2014 auctions were Albie Morkel, Mitchell Starc, Ravi Rampaul, Parthiv Patel, Ashok Dinda, Muttiah Muralitharan, Nic Maddinson, Harshal Patel, Varun Aaron, Vijay Zol and Yuvraj Singh who was the most expensive player fetching a massive 14 crore. They ended up 7th in the points table and didn't qualify for the playoffs in the 2014 IPL.

RCB retained Virat Kohli, AB de Villiers, Chris Gayle, Mitchell Starc, Ashok Dinda, Varun Aaron, Harshal Patel, Yuzvendra Chahal,

Nic Maddinson, Rilee Rossouw, Abu Nechim, Yogesh Takawale, Vijay Zol and Sandeep Warrier for the 2015 Indian Premier League. They also bought Manvinder Bisla and Iqbal Abdulla from Kolkata Knight Riders and Mandeep Singh from Kings XI Punjab during the Transfer Window. They bought Darren Sammy, David Wiese, Adam Milne, Sean Abbott, Subramaniam Badrinath, Jalaj Saxena, Sarfaraz Khan and Dinesh Karthik for 10.5 crore (US$1.4 million) from the 2015 Player Auctions.

- Royal Challengers Bangalore started their season with an unconvincing win against KKR at Kolkata, supported by a knock of 96 by Chris Gayle. But they lost their next three matches in Bangalore to SRH, MI, and CSK. Two great bowling performances ensured RCB secured dominant wins against RR and DD, winning by 9 wickets and 10 wickets respectively. Their next match against RR got washed out after a strong batting performance from RCB. They lost a close match to CSK, but recovered by crushing Kings XI Punjab by 138 runs, supported by a century by Chris Gayle, and a four-wicket haul for Sreenath Aravind and Mitchell Starc. Royal Challengers' good form continued when AB de Villiers and Virat Kohli smashed the highest T20 partnership ever (later beaten by the same pair in IPL 2016) against Mumbai Indians, to secure a good win.
- Later, RCB lost to Kings XI Punjab in a rain affected match, putting their playoff qualification in doubt. They faced SRH in the next match, again affected by rain. Amidst a lot of drama, and stunning performances from Virat Kohli and Gayle, RCB won an unlikely match in Hyderabad. Now, the only way they could be out of the playoffs became very unlikely, yet possible. RCB lost their chance to be placed second in the points table after rain washed out their final match against DD.

They ended the league stage at the third position, with 7 wins from 14 matches. On 20 May, they faced the Rajasthan Royals in the Eliminator and earned a spot in Qualifier 2. However, they lost to the Chennai Super Kings in the Qualifier 2, and ended the season finishing third. AB de Villiers, Virat Kohli and Chris Gayle ended by being the 4th, 5th and 6th highest run scorers of the season respectively, while Yuzvendra Chahal was RCB's highest wicket taker, being the 3rd highest in the season.

- *Virat Kohli set the record for most runs (973) in an IPL season in 2016*

In light of financial scandals involving owner/chairman Vijay Mallya, Amrit Thomas became the chairman of the Royal Challengers. RCB changed the team logo and also became the first team in IPL to adopt different jerseys for home and away matches. Virat Kohli, AB de Villiers, Chris Gayle, Mitchell Starc, David Wiese, Adam Milne, Varun Aaron, Mandeep Singh, Harshal Patel, Kedar Jadhav, Sarfaraz Khan, Sreenath Aravind, Yuzvendra Chahal, and Abu Nechim were retained by RCB for the 2016 Indian Premier League. From player auctions, they bought Shane Watson for 9.5 crore (US$1.3 million), Kane Richardson and Stuart Binny for 2 crore each, and Travis Head and Samuel Badree for 50 lakhs each. Other players that joined the team were Sachin Baby, Iqbal Abdulla, Praveen Dubey, Akshay Karnewar, Vikramjeet Malik and Vikas Tokas. KL Rahul and Parvez Rasool also joined RCB for the IPL 2016 edition.

Royal Challengers Bangalore started their season with a blitz from AB de Villiers and Virat Kohli against SRH at Bangalore, to comfortably win their first match. A bludgeoning century from Quinton de Kock meant RCB lost their second match of the season. Their form deteriorated in the coming matches, winning only one match of the next five. Although, Virat Kohli and AB de Villier's brilliant form, along with the emergence of KL Rahul as an important member of RCB's batting, were positive points. Royal Challengers needed to win at least 6 of their next seven matches to have a chance at qualifying for the playoffs. They won matches against KXIP and Rising Pune Supergiant, the new entrant in the tournament. But a loss against Mumbai Indians meant they needed 4 wins in 4 matches to qualify. Since then, Virat Kohli found himself in a sublime form, with captaincy and the bat. RCB most notably defeated the Gujarat Lions by 144 runs, the highest margin in the IPL history, during this 4 match winning streak. Through other match results, RCB ended at an unlikely second position at the end of the league stage. Virat Kohli dominated the run-scoring list, while Shane Watson and Yuzvendra Chahal collectively topped the wicket taking list at the end of the league stage. They faced the Gujarat Lions in the Qualifier 1 at their home ground, the M. Chinnaswamy Stadium. They won by 4 wickets to make it to their third final in nine seasons. They played the final against SRH, again in Bangalore. RCB lost a hard-fought match by 8 runs, to end as runners up in this ninth season of the IPL. This is the third instance of RCB losing the final in the IPL.

Yuzvendra Chahal and Shane Watson ended second and third respectively on the list for most wickets.

At the launch event of his biography, 'Driven: The Virat Kohli Story' in New Delhi, in October 2016, Kohli announced that RCB would be his permanent IPL franchise that he would play for.

Virat Kohli, AB de Villiers, Chris Gayle, Mitchell Starc, Adam Milne, Mandeep Singh, Harshal Patel, Kedar Jadhav, Sarfaraz Khan, Sreenath Aravind, Yuzvendra Chahal, Shane Watson, Stuart Binny, Travis Head, Samuel Badree, Sachin Baby, Iqbal Abdulla, Praveen Dubey and KL Rahul were retained by RCB for the 2017 Indian Premier League. From the player auctions, they bought Tymal Mills for 12 crore (US$1.6 million), Aniket Chaudhary for 2 crores, Pawan Negi for 1 crore and Billy Stanlake for 30 lakhs. Mitchell Starc dropped out of the season to prepare for the Champions Trophy which led to the management to replace him with Tymal Mills. The team was the worst hit with injuries as their captain Virat Kohli and AB de Villiers did not play for the initial matches which led to the making of Shane Watson as the interim captain. Even their star players KL Rahul and Sarfaraz Khan were ruled out of the season due to their prolonged injuries.

They lost their first match of the season as they were bundled out by 172 and lost by 35 runs to Sunrisers Hyderabad in Hyderabad. But they won their second match against Delhi Daredevils in their home ground. However, they lost the next three matches in a row against Kings XI Punjab, Mumbai Indians and Rising Pune Supergiant respectively. Though AB de Villiers made a quick fire 89 off 46 balls, RCB lost the match against Kings XI Punjab as the other players made 57 dot balls. The match against Mumbai Indians saw Virat Kohli's comeback with a quick 62 off 47 balls and Samuel Badree becoming the 14th player in the IPL history to claim a hat-trick, but they lost the match as Pollard made 70 off 47 balls to win the match for Mumbai Indians. They lost the match against Rising Pune Supergiant by a massive 27 runs. But in their next game against Gujarat Lions, they won by 20 runs and coincidentally Chris Gayle became the first player to score 10,000 runs in T20s.

- However, in their next game against Kolkata Knight Riders, on the day when RCB made 263/5 against Pune Warriors India in 2013 which was the highest IPL score, they were bundled out for 49 all out which is the lowest IPL score and also where no batsman could score 10 runs. They kept losing matches consecutively as they could not make high scores and their big guns – Chris Gayle, Virat Kohli and AB de Villiers failing repeatedly. The pitch in M. Chinnaswamy Stadium was changed from a usual batting to the bowling pitch which made the batsmen struggle for runs. They ended up at the bottom of the table and they changed their squad for each match which was the reason for its downfall. However, they finished their miserable season on a high note after winning against Delhi Daredevils by 10 runs in Delhi. They made low scores like 49 all out against Kolkata Knight Riders, 96/9 against Rising Pune Supergiant and 119 all out against Kings XI Punjab.

- *2018*

In the 2018 IPL, RCB ended up 6th in the points table and didn't qualify for the playoffs.

Ahead of the 2019 IPL, Royal Challengers Bangalore spent 16.4 crores (US$2.4 million) to buy nine players – Shivam Dube, Shimron Hetmyer, Akshdeep Nath, Prayas Barman, Himmat Singh, Gurkeerat Singh Mann, Heinrich Klaasen, Devdutt Padikkal and Milind Kumar. In-between the tournament, one of the best fast bowlers in the game Dale Steyn joined the squad and was crucial for the team's victories. Unfortunately for RCB, he was ruled out of the tournament after playing 3 matches due to a shoulder injury. Despite their hard efforts, RCB failed yet again to deliver in the group-stages. Out of the 14 games played, they won five, lost eight and tied one. Consequently, they ended at the bottom of the points table for the second time (previously in 2017).

A lot of eyes were laid on the Captain of the team Virat Kohli because he was to lead his country in the upcoming Cricket World Cup, this put a lot of pressure on the captain. In spite of this pressure, Kohli scored a total of 464 runs which included one match winning century and two half centuries, making him the second player to reach the milestone of 5,000 runs in the IPL after Chennai Super Kings' All-rounder Suresh Raina.

Even with RCB's disappointing performance in the season, most of their matches were close encounters and their fans were thoroughly entertained. At the end of the 12th season of the IPL franchise, RCB still remains among the three original teams of the franchise (the other two include Kings XI Punjab and Delhi Capitals) which haven't won the IPL trophy yet.

2020

Main article: Royal Challengers Bangalore in 2020

Before the start of 2020 IPL, RCB has released their players: Akshdeep Nath, Colin de Grandhomme, Dale Steyn, Heinrich Klassen, Himmat Singh, Kulwant Khejroliya, Marcus Stoinis, Milind Kumar, Nathan Coulter-Nile, Prayas Ray Barman, Shimron Hetmyer and Tim Southee. During the IPL auction, they added Aaron Finch (4.4 crore), Chris Morris (10 crore), Joshua Philippe (20 lakh),

Kane Richardson (4 crore), Pavan Deshpande (20 lakh), Dale Steyn (2 crore), Shahbaz Ahamad (20 lakh) and Isuru Udana (50 lakh).

- *Team identity*

Vijay Mallya wanted to associate one of his top-selling liquor brands, either McDowell's No.1 or Royal Challenge with the team. The latter was chosen, hence the name.

- Logo

The logo initially consisted the RC emblem in yellow on a circular red base with the black text "Royal Challengers Bangalore" in standard format surrounding the circular logo. The RC crown emblem with the roaring lion placed on the top of the logo was derived from the original Royal Challenge logo. No significant changes took place in the design of the logo except for the replacement of colour yellow with gold from 2009. This logo also had a dotted white circle around the RC emblem. The team also uses an alternate logo for the Game for Green matches where the green plants surround the logo and the text Game for Green is placed below the logo. The logo was redesigned in 2016 with the inclusion of black as a secondary color. The lion emblem in the crest was enlarged and the shield was omitted in the new design. In 2020, a new logo was unveiled featuring a bigger lion and the crown returning from the previous logo. The RC emblem was omitted for this crest.

Jersey

The jersey colors of the team in 2008 were red and golden yellow, the same as the unofficial Kannada flag, with player names printed in white and numbers printed in black in the rear. Yellow was eliminated in future seasons and was replaced with gold. Starting from 2010, blue was introduced on the apparel as a tertiary colour. The jersey design saw tweaks every season, major being the one for 2014 where blue dominated over gold. From 2014, the player names and numbers were printed in gold. As of 2015, more yellowish shade of gold is being used on the jerseys. The blue was eliminated in 2016 and was replaced by black as the third colour in the two versions of the jersey; one for home matches and the other for away ones. From 2020, black was replaced with a shade between dark blue and black. Reebok manufactured kits for the team from 2008 to 2014 and Adidas supplied the kits in 2015. Zeven manufactures the kits for the team from 2016.

- Theme song

The theme song of the team for the 2008 season was "Jeetenge Hum Shaan Se". The team anthem, "Game for More" was created for the 2009 season. The music was composed by Amit Trivedi and written by Anshu Sharma. A new anthem, "Here We Go The Royal Challengers" was created for the 2013 season and was used till 2015. The anthem "Play Bold" was composed by Salim–Sulaiman, sung by Siddharth Basrur and was released in 2016 during the launch of jerseys for the season. For 2017, the same anthem was recomposed and sung by Anand Bhaskar in 6 languages – English, Kannada, Telugu, Bengali, Marathi and Punjabi.

- Ambassadors

Katrina Kaif was roped in as the brand ambassador for the team in 2008, but later stepped down due to her prior commitments with filmmakers. Deepika Padukone, Ramya, Puneeth Rajkumar, Upendra and Ganesh have been the ambassadors for the team in the initial seasons.Shiva Rajkumar is the brand Ambassador for the season 11.

CHAPTER THREE

Let's Know About Cricket

- Cricket

Cricket is a bat-and-ball game played between two teams of eleven players on a field at the centre of which is a 22-yard (20-metre) pitch with a wicket at each end, each comprising two bails balanced on three stumps. The game proceeds when a player on the fielding team, called the bowler, "bowls" (propels) the ball from one end of the pitch towards the wicket at the other end. The batting side's players score runs by striking the bowled ball with a bat and running between the wickets, while the bowling side tries to prevent this by keeping the ball within the field and getting it to either wicket, and dismiss each batter (so they are "out"). Means of dismissal include being bowled, when the ball hits the stumps and dislodges the bails, and by the fielding side either catching a hit ball before it touches the ground, or hitting a wicket with the ball before a batter can cross the crease line in front of the wicket to complete a run. When ten batters have been dismissed, the innings ends and the teams swap roles. The game is adjudicated by two umpires, aided by a third umpire and match referee in international matches.

Forms of cricket range from Twenty20, with each team batting for a single innings of 20 overs and the game generally lasting three hours, to Test matches played over five days. Traditionally cricketers play in all-white kit, but in limited overs cricket they wear club or team colours. In addition to the basic kit, some players wear protective gear to prevent injury caused by the ball, which is a hard, solid spheroid made of compressed leather with a slightly raised sewn seam enclosing a cork core layered with tightly wound string.

The earliest reference to cricket is in South East England in the mid-16th century. It spread globally with the expansion of the British Empire, with the first international matches in the second half of the 19th century. The game's governing body is the International Cricket Council (ICC), which has over 100 members, twelve of which are full members who play Test matches. The game's rules, the Laws of Cricket, are maintained by Marylebone Cricket Club (MCC) in London. The sport is followed primarily in South Asia, Australasia, the United Kingdom, southern Africa and the West Indies.Women's cricket, which is organised and played separately, has also achieved international standard. The most successful side playing international cricket is Australia, which has won seven One Day International trophies, including five World Cups, more than any other country and has been the top-rated Test side more than any other country.

- History of cricket to 1725

A medieval "club ball" game involving an underhand bowl towards a batter. Ball catchers are shown positioning themselves to catch a ball. Detail from the Canticles of Holy Mary, 13th century.

Cricket is one of many games in the "club ball" sphere that basically involve hitting a ball with a hand-held implement; others include baseball (which shares many similarities with cricket, both belonging in the more specific bat-and-ball games category), golf, hockey, tennis, squash, badminton and table tennis. In cricket's case, a key difference is the existence of a solid target structure, the wicket (originally, it is thought, a "wicket gate" through which sheep were herded), that the batter must defend. The cricket historian Harry Altham identified three "groups" of "club ball" games: the "hockey group", in which the ball is driven to and fro between two targets (the goals); the "golf group", in which the ball is driven towards an undefended target (the hole); and the "cricket group", in which "the ball is aimed at a mark (the wicket) and driven away from it".

It is generally believed that cricket originated as a children's game in the south-eastern counties of England, sometime during the medieval period.Although there are claims for prior dates, the earliest definite reference to cricket being played comes from evidence given at a court case in Guildford in January 1597 (Old Style), equating to January 1598 in the modern calendar. The case concerned ownership of a certain plot of land and the court heard the testimony of a 59-year-old coroner, John Derrick, who gave witness that.

Being a scholler in the ffree schoole of Guldeford hee and diverse of his fellows did runne and play there at creckett and other plaies.

Given Derrick's age, it was about half a century earlier when he was at school and so it is certain that cricket was being played c. 1550 by boys in Surrey. The view that it was originally a children's game is reinforced by Randle Cotgrave's 1611 English-French dictionary in which he defined the noun "crosse" as "the crooked staff wherewith boys play at cricket" and the verb form "crosser" as "to play at cricket".

One possible source for the sport's name is the Old English word "cryce" (or "cricc") meaning a crutch or staff. In Samuel Johnson's Dictionary, he derived cricket from "cryce, Saxon, a stick". In Old French, the word "criquet" seems to have meant a kind of club or stick. Given the strong medieval trade connections between south-east England and the County of Flanders when the latter belonged to the Duchy of Burgundy, the name may have been derived from the Middle Dutch (in use in Flanders at the time) "krick"(-e), meaning a stick (crook). Another possible source is the Middle Dutch word "krickstoel", meaning a long low stool used for kneeling in church and which resembled the long low wicket with two stumps used in early cricket. According to Heiner Gillmeister, a European language expert of Bonn University, "cricket" derives from the Middle Dutch phrase for hockey, met de (krik ket)sen (i.e., "with the stick chase"). Gillmeister has suggested that not only the name but also the sport itself may be of Flemish origin.

- Growth of amateur and professional cricket in England

Evolution of the cricket bat. The original "hockey stick" (left) evolved into the straight bat from c. 1760 when pitched delivery bowling began.

Although the main object of the game has always been to score the most runs, the early form of cricket differed from the modern game in certain key technical aspects; the North American variant of cricket known as wicket retained many of these aspects. The ball was bowled underarm by the bowler and along the ground towards a batter armed with a bat that in shape resembled a hockey stick; the batter defended a low, two-stump wicket; and runs were called notches because the scorers recorded them by notching tally sticks.

In 1611, the year Cotgrave's dictionary was published, ecclesiastical court records at Sidlesham in Sussex state that two parishioners, Bartholomew Wyatt and Richard Latter, failed to attend church on Easter Sunday because they were playing cricket. They were fined 12d each and ordered to do penance.This is the earliest mention of adult participation in cricket and it was around the same time that the earliest known organised inter-parish or village match was played – at Chevening, Kent. In 1624, a player called Jasper Vinall died after he was accidentally struck on the head during a match between two parish teams in Sussex.

Cricket remained a low-key local pursuit for much of the 17th century. It is known, through numerous references found in the records of ecclesiastical court cases, to have been proscribed at times by the Puritans before and during the Commonwealth. The problem was nearly always the issue of Sunday play as the Puritans considered cricket to be "profane" if played on the Sabbath, especially if large crowds or gambling were involved.

According to the social historian Derek Birley, there was a "great upsurge of sport after the Restoration" in 1660. Gambling on sport became a problem significant enough for Parliament to pass the 1664 Gambling Act, limiting stakes to £100 which was, in any case, a colossal sum exceeding the annual income of 99% of the population. Along with prizefighting, horse racing and blood sports, cricket was perceived to be a gambling sport.Rich patrons made matches for high stakes, forming teams in which they engaged the first professional players.By the end of the century, cricket had developed into a major sport that was spreading throughout England and was already being taken abroad by English mariners and colonisers – the earliest reference to cricket overseas is dated 1676. A 1697 newspaper report survives of "a great cricket match" played in Sussex "for fifty guineas apiece" – this is the earliest known contest that is generally considered a First Class match.

- The patrons, and other players from the social class known as the "gentry", began to classify themselves as "amateurs" to establish a clear distinction from the professionals, who were invariably members of the working class, even to the point of having separate changing and dining facilities. The gentry, including such high-ranking nobles as the Dukes of Richmond, exerted their honour code of noblesse oblige to claim rights of leadership in any sporting contests they took part in, especially as it was necessary for them to play alongside their "social inferiors" if they were to win their bets. In time, a perception took hold that the typical amateur who played in first-class cricket, until 1962 when amateurism was abolished, was someone with a public school education who had then gone to one of Cambridge or Oxford University – society insisted that such people were "officers and gentlemen" whose destiny was to provide leadership. In a purely financial sense, the cricketing amateur would theoretically claim expenses for playing while his professional counterpart played under contract and was paid a wage or match fee; in practice, many amateurs claimed more than actual expenditure and the derisive term "shamateur" was coined to describe the practice.

- The Young Cricketer, 1768

The game underwent major development in the 18th century to become England's national sport.Its success was underwritten by the twin necessities of patronage and betting. Cricket was prominent in London as early as 1707 and, in the middle years of the century, large crowds flocked to matches on the Artillery Ground in Finsbury. The single wicket form of the sport attracted huge crowds and wagers to match, its popularity peaking in the 1748 season. Bowling underwent an evolution around 1760 when bowlers began to pitch the ball instead of rolling or skimming it towards the batter. This caused a revolution in bat design because, to deal with the bouncing ball, it was necessary to introduce the modern straight bat in place of the old "hockey stick" shape.

The Hambledon Club was founded in the 1760s and, for the next twenty years until the formation of Marylebone Cricket Club (MCC) and the opening of Lord's Old Ground in 1787, Hambledon was both the game's greatest club and its focal point. MCC quickly became the sport's premier club and the custodian of the Laws of Cricket. New Laws introduced in the latter part of the 18th century included the three stump wicket and leg before wicket (lbw).

The 19th century saw underarm bowling superseded by first roundarm and then overarm bowling. Both developments were controversial.Organisation of the game at county level led to the creation of the county clubs, starting with Sussex in 1839. In December 1889, the eight leading county clubs formed the official County Championship, which began in 1890.

The most famous player of the 19th century was W. G. Grace, who started his long and influential career in 1865. It was especially during the career of Grace that the distinction between amateurs and professionals became blurred by the existence of players like him who were nominally amateur but, in terms of their financial gain, de facto professional. Grace himself was said to have been paid more money for playing cricket than any professional.

The last two decades before the First World War have been called the "Golden Age of cricket". It is a nostalgic name prompted by the collective sense of loss resulting from the war, but the period did produce some great players and memorable matches, especially as organised competition at county and Test level developed.

- Cricket becomes an international sport

In 1844, the first-ever international match took place between the United States and Canada. In 1859, a team of English players went to North America on the first overseas tour. Meanwhile, the British Empire had been instrumental in spreading the game overseas and by the middle of the 19th century it had become well established in Australia, the Caribbean, India, Pakistan, New Zealand, North America and South Africa.

In 1862, an English team made the first tour of Australia. The first Australian team to travel overseas consisted of Aboriginal stockmen who toured England in 1868. The first One Day International match was played on 5 January 1971 between Australia and England at the Melbourne Cricket Ground.

In 1876–77, an England team took part in what was retrospectively recognised as the first-ever Test match at the Melbourne Cricket Ground against Australia. The rivalry between England and Australia gave birth to The Ashes in 1882, and this has remained Test cricket's most famous contest. Test cricket began to expand in 1888–89 when South Africa played England.

- World cricket in the 20th century

The inter-war years were dominated by Australia's Don Bradman, statistically the greatest Test batter of all time. Test cricket continued to expand during the 20th century with the addition of the West Indies (1928), New Zealand (1930) and India (1932) before the Second World War and then Pakistan (1952), Sri Lanka (1982), Zimbabwe (1992), Bangladesh (2000), Ireland and Afghanistan (both 2018) in the post-war period. South Africa was banned from international cricket from 1970 to 1992 as part of the apartheid boycott.

- The rise of limited overs cricket

Cricket entered a new era in 1963 when English counties introduced the limited overs variant. As it was sure to produce a result, limited overs cricket was lucrative and the number of matches increased. The first Limited Overs International was played in 1971 and the governing International Cricket Council (ICC), seeing its potential, staged the first limited overs Cricket World Cup in 1975. In the 21st century, a new limited overs form, Twenty20, made an immediate impact. On 22 June 2017, Afghanistan and Ireland became the 11th and 12th ICC full members, enabling them to play Test cricket.

- A typical cricket field.

In cricket, the rules of the game are specified in a code called The Laws of Cricket (hereinafter called "the Laws") which has a global remit. There are 42 Laws (always written with a capital "L"). The earliest known version of the code was drafted in 1744 and, since 1788, it has been owned and maintained by its custodian, the Marylebone Cricket Club (MCC) in London.

- Playing area

Cricket is a bat-and-ball game played on a cricket field between two teams of eleven players each. The field is usually circular or oval in shape and the edge of the playing area is marked by a boundary, which may be a fence, part of the stands, a rope, a painted line or a combination of these; the boundary must if possible be marked along its entire length.

In the approximate centre of the field is a rectangular pitch (see image, below) on which a wooden target called a wicket is sited at each end; the wickets are placed 22 yards (20 m) apart. The pitch is a flat surface 10 feet (3.0 m) wide, with very short grass that tends to be worn away as the game progresses (cricket can also be played on artificial surfaces, notably matting). Each wicket is made of three wooden stumps topped by two bails.

- Cricket pitch and creases

As illustrated above, the pitch is marked at each end with four white painted lines: a bowling crease, a popping crease and two return creases. The three stumps are aligned centrally on the bowling crease, which is eight feet eight inches long. The popping crease is drawn four feet in front of the bowling crease and parallel to it; although it is drawn as a twelve-foot line (six feet either side of the wicket), it is, in fact, unlimited in length. The return creases are drawn at right angles to the popping crease so that they intersect the ends of the bowling crease; each return crease is drawn as an eight-foot line, so that it extends four feet behind the bowling crease, but is also, in fact, unlimited in length.

Before a match begins, the team captains (who are also players) toss a coin to decide which team will bat first and so take the first innings. Innings is the term used for each phase of play in the match.In each innings, one team bats, attempting to score runs, while the other team bowls and fields the ball, attempting to restrict the scoring and dismiss the batters. When the first innings ends, the teams change roles; there can be two to four innings depending upon the type of match. A match with four scheduled innings is played over three to five days; a match with two scheduled innings is usually completed in a single day. During an innings, all eleven members of the fielding team take the field, but usually only two members of the batting team are on the field at any given time.

The exception to this is if a batter has any type of illness or injury restricting his or her ability to run, in this case the batter is allowed a runner who can run between the wickets when the batter hits a scoring run or runs,though this does not apply in international cricket. The order of batters is usually announced just before the match, but it can be varied.

The main objective of each team is to score more runs than their opponents but, in some forms of cricket, it is also necessary to dismiss all of the opposition batters in their final innings in order to win the match, which would otherwise be drawn. If the team batting last is all out having scored fewer runs than their opponents, they are said to have "lost by n runs" (where n is the difference between the aggregate number of runs scored by the teams). If the team that bats last scores enough runs to win, it is said to have "won by n wickets", where n is the number of wickets left to fall. For example, a team that passes its opponents‘ total having lost six wickets (i.e., six of their batters have been dismissed) have won the match "by four wickets".

In a two-innings-a-side match, one team's combined first and second innings total may be less than the other side's first innings total. The team with the greater score is then said to have "won by an innings and n runs", and does not need to bat again: n is the difference between the two teams' aggregate scores. If the team batting last is all out, and both sides have scored the same number of runs, then the match is a tie; this result is quite rare in matches of two innings a side with only 62 happening in first-class matches from the earliest known instance in 1741 until January 2017. In the traditional form of the game, if the time allotted for the match expires before either side can win, then the game is declared a draw.

If the match has only a single innings per side, then a maximum number of overs applies to each innings. Such a match is called a "limited overs" or "one-day" match, and the side scoring more runs wins regardless of the number of wickets lost, so that a draw cannot occur. In some cases, ties are broken by having each team bat for a one-over innings known as a Super Over; subsequent Super Overs may be played if the first Super Over ends in a tie. If this kind of match is temporarily interrupted by bad weather, then a complex mathematical formula, known as the Duckworth–Lewis–Stern method after its developers, is often used to recalculate a new target score. A one-day match can also be declared a "no-result" if fewer than a previously agreed number of overs have been bowled by either team, in circumstances that make normal resumption of play impossible; for example, wet weather.

In all forms of cricket, the umpires can abandon the match if bad light or rain makes it impossible to continue. There have been instances of entire matches, even Test matches scheduled to be played over five days, being lost to bad weather without a ball being bowled: for example, the third Test of the 1970/71 series in Australia.

- Innings

The innings (ending with 's' in both singular and plural form) is the term used for each phase of play during a match. Depending on the type of match being played, each team has either one or two innings. Sometimes all eleven members of the batting side take a turn to bat but, for various reasons, an innings can end before they have all done so. The innings terminates if the batting team is "all out", a term defined by the Laws: "at the fall of a wicket or the retirement of a batter, further balls remain to be bowled but no further batter is available to come in". In this situation, one of the batters has not been dismissed and is termed not out; this is because he has no partners left and there must always be two active batters while the innings is in progress.

- An innings may end early while there are still two not out batters

the batting team's captain may declare the innings closed even though some of his players have not had a turn to bat: this is a tactical decision by the captain, usually because he believes his team have scored sufficient runs and need time to dismiss the opposition in their innings

the set number of overs (i.e., in a limited overs match) have been bowled

the match has ended prematurely due to bad weather or running out of time

in the final innings of the match, the batting side has reached its target and won the game.

- Overs

The Laws state that, throughout an innings, "the ball shall be bowled from each end alternately in overs of 6 balls". The name "over" came about because the umpire calls "Over!" when six balls have been bowled. At this point, another bowler is deployed at the other end, and the fielding side changes ends while the batters do not. A bowler cannot bowl two successive overs, although a bowler can (and usually does) bowl alternate overs, from the same end, for several overs which are termed a "spell". The batters do not change ends at the end of the over, and so the one who was non-striker is now the striker and vice versa. The umpires also change positions so that the one who was at "square leg" now stands behind the wicket at the non-striker's end and vice versa.

- Clothing and equipment

English cricketer W. G. Grace "taking guard" in 1883. His pads and bat are very similar to those used today. The gloves have evolved somewhat. Many modern players use more defensive equipment than were available to Grace, most notably helmets and arm guards.

The wicket-keeper (a specialised fielder behind the batter) and the batters wear protective gear because of the hardness of the ball, which can be delivered at speeds of more than 145 kilometres per hour (90 mph) and presents a major health and safety concern.

Protective clothing includes pads (designed to protect the knees and shins), batting gloves or wicket-keeper's gloves for the hands, a safety helmet for the head and a box for male players inside the trousers (to protect the crotch area). Some batters wear additional padding inside their shirts and trousers such as thigh pads, arm pads, rib protectors and shoulder pads. The only fielders allowed to wear protective gear are those in positions very close to the batter (i.e., if they are alongside or in front of him), but they cannot wear gloves or external leg guards.

Subject to certain variations, on-field clothing generally includes a collared shirt with short or long sleeves; long trousers; woolen pullover (if needed); cricket cap (for fielding) or a safety helmet; and spiked shoes or boots to increase traction. The kit is traditionally all white and this remains the case in Test and first-class cricket but, in limited overs cricket, team colours are worn instead.

- Bat and ball

Two types of cricket ball, both of the same size:

i) A used white ball. White balls are mainly used in limited overs cricket, especially in matches played at night, under floodlights (left).

ii) A used red ball. Red balls are used in Test cricket, first-class cricket and some other forms of cricket (right).

The essence of the sport is that a bowler delivers (i.e., bowls) the ball from his or her end of the pitch towards the batter who, armed with a bat, is "on strike" at the other end (see next sub-section: Basic gameplay).

The bat is made of wood, usually Salix alba (white willow), and has the shape of a blade topped by a cylindrical handle. The blade must not be more than 4.25 inches (10.8 cm) wide and the total length of the bat not more than 38 inches (97 cm). There is no standard for the weight, which is usually between 2 lb 7 oz and 3 lb (1.1 and 1.4 kg).

The ball is a hard leather-seamed spheroid, with a circumference of 9 inches (23 cm). The ball has a "seam": six rows of stitches attaching the leather shell of the ball to the string and cork interior. The seam on a new ball is prominent and helps the bowler propel it in a less predictable manner. During matches, the quality of the ball deteriorates to a point where it is no longer usable; during the course of this deterioration, its behaviour in flight will change and can influence the outcome of the match. Players will, therefore, attempt to modify the ball's behaviour by modifying its physical properties. Polishing the ball and wetting it with sweat or saliva is legal, even when the polishing is deliberately done on one side only to increase the ball's swing through the air, but the acts of rubbing other substances into the ball, scratching the surface or picking at the seam are illegal ball tampering.

- Player roles

Basic gameplay: bowler to batter

During normal play, thirteen players and two umpires are on the field. Two of the players are batters and the rest are all eleven members of the fielding team. The other nine players in the batting team are off the field in the pavilion. The image with overlay below shows what is happening when a ball is being bowled and which of the personnel are on or close to the pitch.

- Return crease

In the photo, the two batters (3 & 8; wearing yellow) have taken position at each end of the pitch (6). Three members of the fielding team (4, 10 & 11; wearing dark blue) are in shot. One of the two umpires (1; wearing white hat) is stationed behind the wicket (2) at the bowler's (4) end of the pitch. The bowler (4) is bowling the ball (5) from his end of the pitch to the batter at the other end who is called the "striker". The other batter (3) at the bowling end is called the "non-striker". The wicket-keeper (10), who is a specialist, is positioned behind the striker's wicket (9) and behind him stands one of the fielders in a position called "first slip" (11). While the bowler and the first slip are wearing conventional kit only, the two batters and the wicket-keeper are wearing protective gear including safety helmets, padded gloves and leg guards (pads).

While the umpire (1) in shot stands at the bowler's end of the pitch, his colleague stands in the outfield, usually in or near the fielding position called "square leg", so that he is in line with the popping crease (7) at the striker's end of the pitch. The bowling crease (not numbered) is the one on which the wicket is located between the return creases (12). The bowler (4) intends to hit the wicket (9) with the ball (5) or, at least, to prevent the striker (8) from scoring runs. The striker (8) intends, by using his bat, to defend his wicket and, if possible, to hit the ball away from the pitch in order to score runs.

Some players are skilled in both batting and bowling, or as either or these as well as wicket-keeping, so are termed all-rounders. Bowlers are classified according to their style, generally as fast bowlers, seam bowlers or spinners. Batters are classified according to whether they are right-handed or left-handed.

- Fielding

Of the eleven fielders, three are in shot in the image above. The other eight are elsewhere on the field, their positions determined on a tactical basis by the captain or the bowler. Fielders often change position between deliveries, again as directed by the captain or bowler.

If a fielder is injured or becomes ill during a match, a substitute is allowed to field instead of him, but the substitute cannot bowl or act as a captain, except in the case of concussion substitutes in international cricket. The substitute leaves the field when the injured player is fit to return. The Laws of Cricket were updated in 2017 to allow substitutes to act as wicket-keepers.

- Bowling and dismissal

Glenn McGrath of Australia holds the world record for most wickets in the Cricket World Cup.

Most bowlers are considered specialists in that they are selected for the team because of their skill as a bowler, although some are all-rounders and even specialist batters bowl occasionally. The specialists bowl several times during an innings but may not bowl two overs consecutively. If the captain wants a bowler to "change ends", another bowler must temporarily fill in so that the change is not immediate.

A bowler reaches his delivery stride by means of a "run-up" and an over is deemed to have begun when the bowler starts his run-up for the first delivery of that over, the ball then being "in play".

Fast bowlers, needing momentum, take a lengthy run up while bowlers with a slow delivery take no more than a couple of steps before bowling. The fastest bowlers can deliver the ball at a speed of over 145 kilometres per hour (90 mph) and they sometimes rely on sheer speed to try to defeat the batter, who is forced to react very quickly.

Other fast bowlers rely on a mixture of speed and guile by making the ball seam or swing (i.e. curve) in flight. This type of delivery can deceive a batter into miscuing his shot, for example, so that the ball just touches the edge of the bat and can then be "caught behind" by the wicket-keeper or a slip fielder. At the other end of the bowling scale is the spin bowler who bowls at a relatively slow pace and relies entirely on guile to deceive the batter. A spinner will often "buy his wicket" by "tossing one up" (in a slower, steeper parabolic path) to lure the batter into making a poor shot. The batter has to be very wary of such deliveries as they are often "flighted" or spun so that the ball will not behave quite as he expects and he could be "trapped" into getting himself out. In between the pacemen and the spinners are the medium paced seamers who rely on persistent accuracy to try to contain the rate of scoring and wear down the batter's concentration.

There are nine ways in which a batter can be dismissed: five relatively common and four extremely rare. The common forms of dismissal are bowled, caught, leg before wicket (lbw), run out and stumped. Rare methods are hit wicket,hit the ball twice, obstructing the field and timed out. The Laws state that the fielding team, usually the bowler in practice, must appeal for a dismissal before the umpire can give his decision. If the batter is out, the umpire raises a forefinger and says "Out!"; otherwise, he will shake his head and say "Not out".There is, effectively, a tenth method of dismissal, retired out, which is not an on-field dismissal as such but rather a retrospective one for which no fielder is credited.

- Batting, runs and extras

The directions in which a right-handed batter, facing down the page, intends to send the ball when playing various cricketing shots. The diagram for a left-handed batter is a mirror image of this one.

Batters take turns to bat via a batting order which is decided beforehand by the team captain and presented to the umpires, though the order remains flexible when the captain officially nominates the team. Substitute batters are generally not allowed, except in the case of concussion substitutes in international cricket.

In order to begin batting the batter first adopts a batting stance. Standardly, this involves adopting a slight crouch with the feet pointing across the front of the wicket, looking in the direction of the bowler, and holding the bat so it passes over the feet and so its tip can rest on the ground near to the toes of the back foot.

A skilled batter can use a wide array of "shots" or "strokes" in both defensive and attacking mode. The idea is to hit the ball to the best effect with the flat surface of the bat's blade. If the ball touches the side of the bat it is called an "edge". The batter does not have to play a shot and can allow the ball to go through to the wicketkeeper. Equally, he does not have to attempt a run when he hits the ball with his bat. Batters do not always seek to hit the ball as hard as possible, and a good player can score runs just by making a deft stroke with a turn of the wrists or by simply "blocking" the ball but directing it away from fielders so that he has time to take a run. A wide variety of shots are played, the batter's repertoire including strokes named according to the style of swing and the direction aimed: e.g., "cut", "drive", "hook", "pull".

The batter on strike (i.e. the "striker") must prevent the ball hitting the wicket, and try to score runs by hitting the ball with his bat so that he and his partner have time to run from one end of the pitch to the other before the fielding side can return the ball. To register a run, both runners must touch the ground behind the popping crease with either their bats or their bodies (the batters carry their bats as they run). Each completed run increments the score of both the team and the striker.

- Sachin Tendulkar is the only player to have scored one hundred international centuries

The decision to attempt a run is ideally made by the batter who has the better view of the ball's progress, and this is communicated by calling: usually "yes", "no" or "wait". More than one run can be scored from a single hit: hits worth one to three runs are common, but the size of the field is such that it is usually difficult to run four or more. To compensate for this, hits that reach the boundary of the field are automatically awarded four runs if the ball touches the ground en route to the boundary or six runs if the ball clears the boundary without touching the ground within the boundary. In these cases the batters do not need to run. Hits for five are unusual and generally rely on the help of "overthrows" by a fielder returning the ball. If an odd number of runs is scored by the striker, the two batters have changed ends, and the one who was non-striker is now the striker. Only the striker can score individual runs, but all runs are added to the team's total.

Additional runs can be gained by the batting team as extras (called "sundries" in Australia) due to errors made by the fielding side. This is achieved in four ways: no-ball, a penalty of one extra conceded by the bowler if he breaks the rules; wide, a penalty of one extra conceded by the bowler if he bowls so that the ball is out of the batter's reach bye, an extra awarded if the batter misses the ball and it goes past the wicket-keeper and gives the batters time to run in the conventional way leg bye, as for a bye except that the ball has hit the batter's body, though not his bat. If the bowler has conceded a no-ball or a wide, his team incurs an additional penalty because that ball (i.e., delivery) has to be bowled again and hence the batting side has the opportunity to score more runs from this extra ball.

- Specialist roles

Captain (cricket) and Wicket-keeper

The captain is often the most experienced player in the team, certainly the most tactically astute, and can possess any of the main skillsets as a batter, a bowler or a wicket-keeper. Within the Laws, the captain has certain responsibilities in terms of nominating his players to the umpires before the match and ensuring that his players conduct themselves "within the spirit and traditions of the game as well as within the Laws".

The wicket-keeper (sometimes called simply the "keeper") is a specialist fielder subject to various rules within the Laws about his equipment and demeanour. He is the only member of the fielding side who can effect a stumping and is the only one permitted to wear gloves and external leg guards. Depending on their primary skills, the other ten players in the team tend to be classified as specialist batters or specialist bowlers. Generally, a team will include five or six specialist batters and four or five specialist bowlers, plus the wicket-keeper.

- Umpires and scorers

Umpire (cricket), Scoring (cricket), and Cricket statistics

An umpire signals a decision to the scorers

The game on the field is regulated by the two umpires, one of whom stands behind the wicket at the bowler's end, the other in a position called "square leg" which is about 15–20 metres away from the batter on strike and in line with the popping crease on which he is taking guard. The umpires have several responsibilities including adjudication on whether a ball has been correctly bowled (i.e., not a no-ball or a wide); when a run is scored; whether a batter is out (the fielding side must first appeal to the umpire, usually with the phrase "How's that?" or "Owzat?"); when intervals start and end; and the suitability of the pitch, field and weather for playing the game. The umpires are authorised to interrupt or even abandon a match due to circumstances likely to endanger the players, such as a damp pitch or deterioration of the light.

Off the field in televised matches, there is usually a third umpire who can make decisions on certain incidents with the aid of video evidence. The third umpire is mandatory under the playing conditions for Test and Limited Overs International matches played between two ICC full member countries. These matches also have a match referee whose job is to ensure that play is within the Laws and the spirit of the game.

The match details, including runs and dismissals, are recorded by two official scorers, one representing each team. The scorers are directed by the hand signals of an umpire . For example, the umpire raises a forefinger to signal that the batter is out (has been dismissed); he raises both arms above his head if the batter has hit the ball for six runs. The scorers are required by the Laws to record all runs scored, wickets taken and overs bowled; in practice, they also note significant amounts of additional data relating to the game.

A match's statistics are summarised on a scorecard. Prior to the popularisation of scorecards, most scoring was done by men sitting on vantage points cuttings notches on tally sticks and runs were originally called notches.According to Rowland Bowen, the earliest known scorecard templates were introduced in 1776 by T. Pratt of Sevenoaks and soon came into general use.It is believed that scorecards were printed and sold at Lord's for the first time in 1846.

- thank you for buy & read this book

  have a great day of your
  from : Mr Vivek Kumar Pandey

9 798885 463614

Printed by Libri Plureos GmbH in Hamburg,
Germany